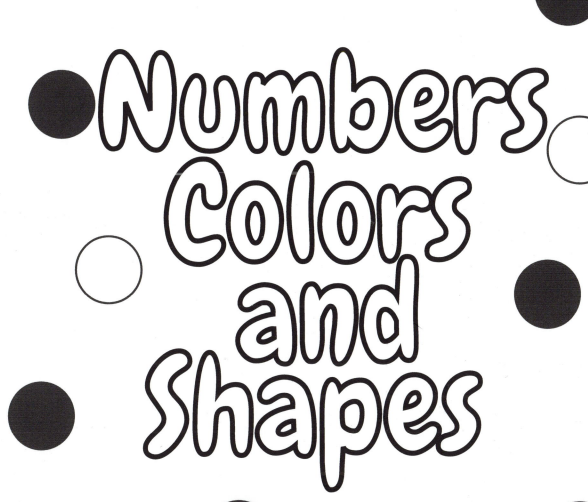

Numbers Colors and Shapes

Zero

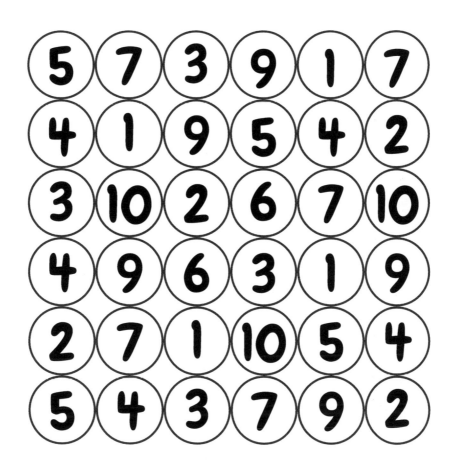

5	7	3	9	1	7
4	1	9	5	4	2
3	10	2	6	7	10
4	9	6	3	1	9
2	7	1	10	5	4
5	4	3	7	9	2

Find Color and Count

0

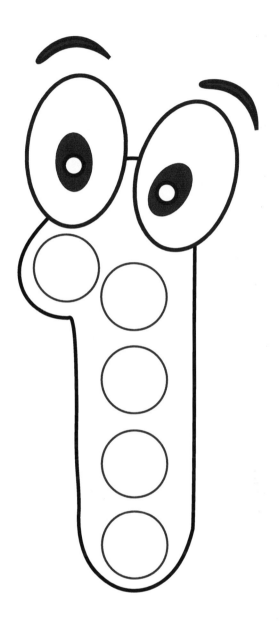

One

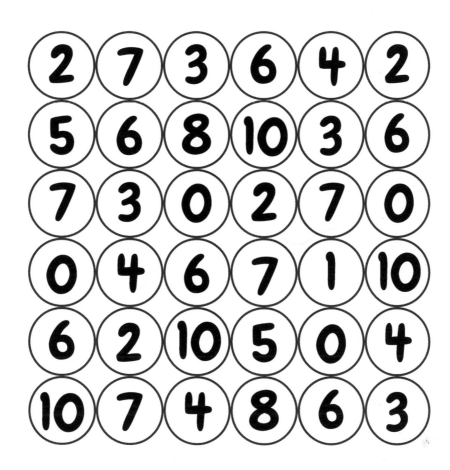

Find Color and Count 1

Two

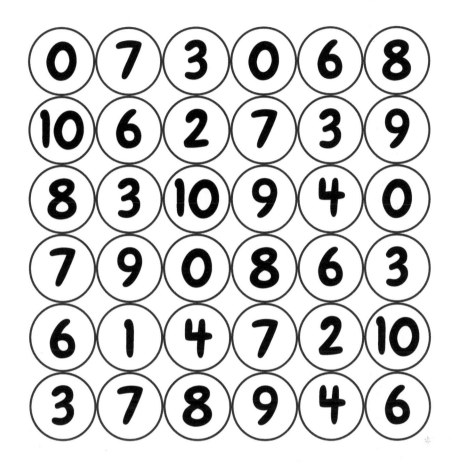

Find Color and Count 2

Three

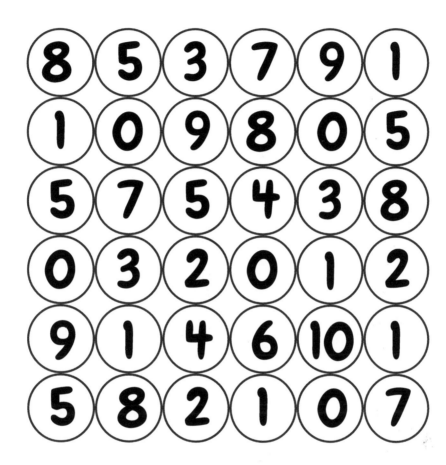

Find Color and Count 3

Four

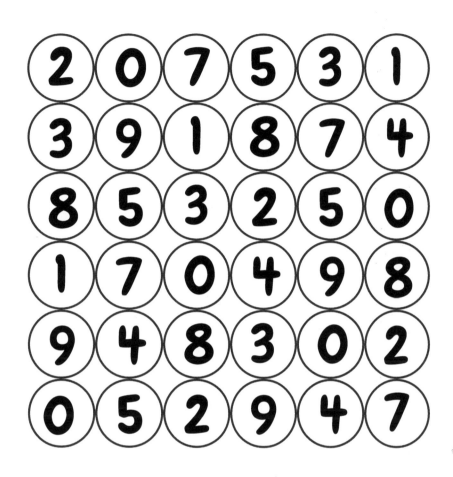

Find Color and Count 4

Five

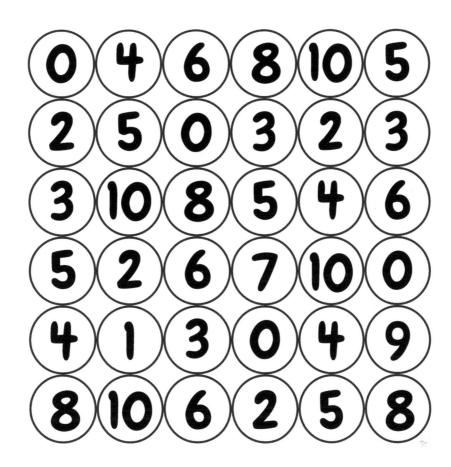

0	4	6	8	10	5
2	5	0	3	2	3
3	10	8	5	4	6
5	2	6	7	10	0
4	1	3	0	4	9
8	10	6	2	5	8

Find Color and Count 5

Six

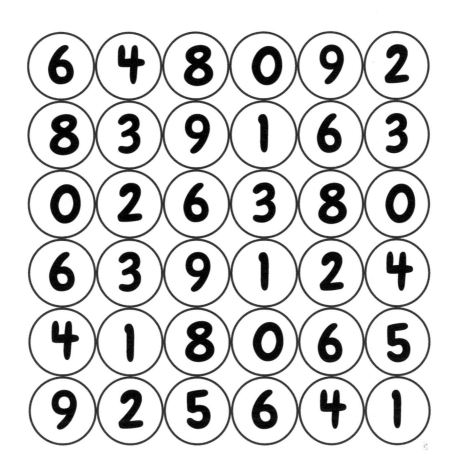

Find Color and Count 6

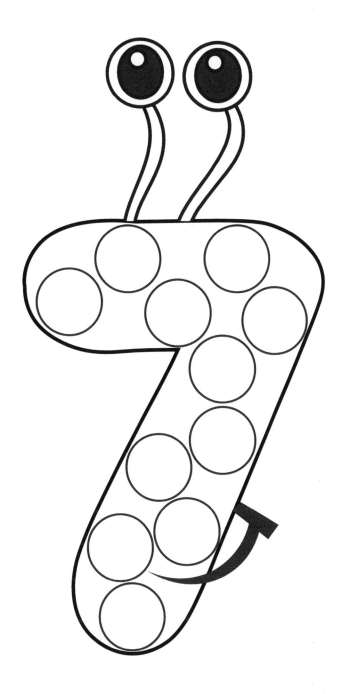

Seven

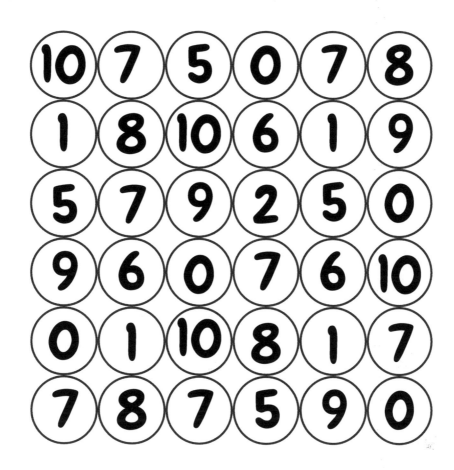

Find Color and Count 7

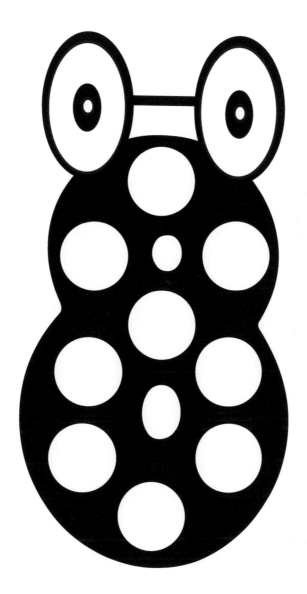

Eight

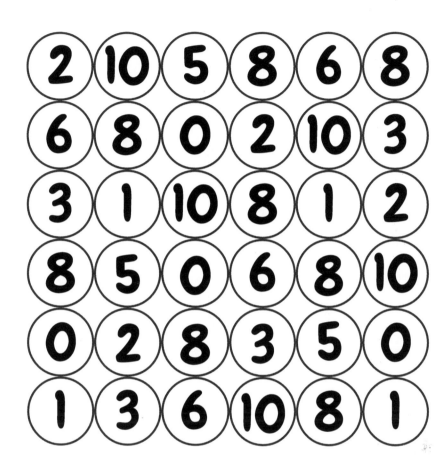

Find Color and Count

8

Nine

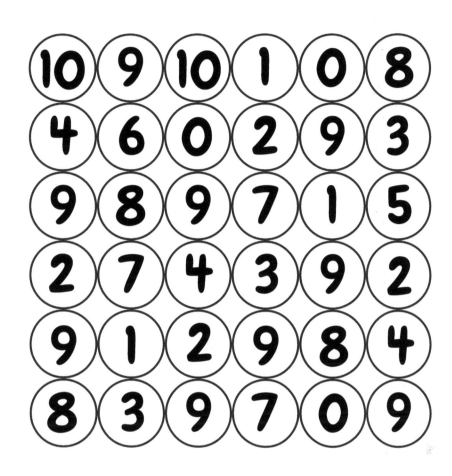

Find Color and Count 9

Ten

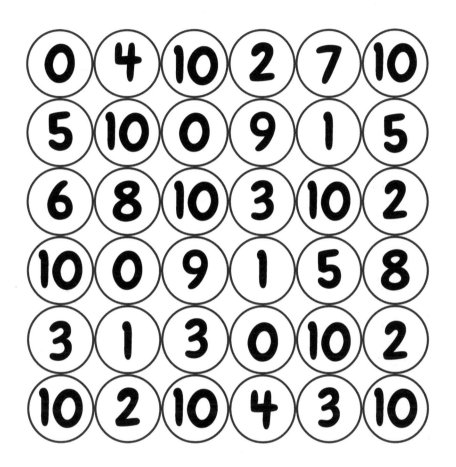

Find Color and Count 10

Color: gray

Color: blue

Color: yellow

Color: red

Color: green

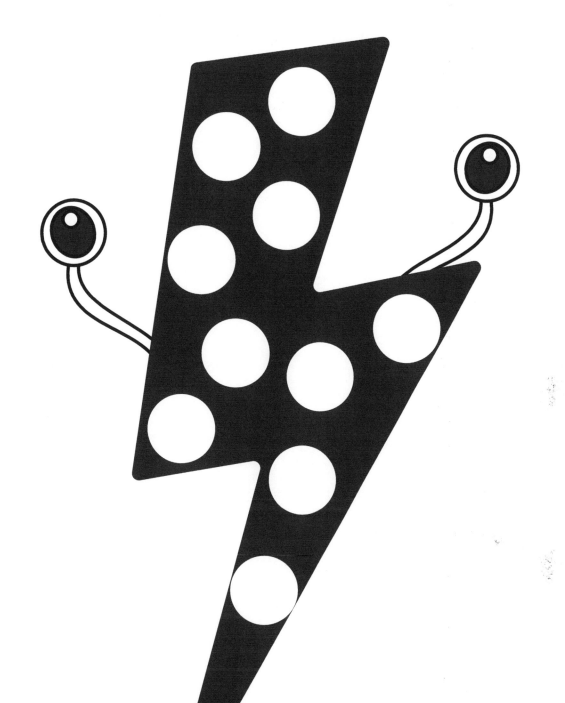

Color: violet

Color: orange

Color: brown

Color: pink

Color: black

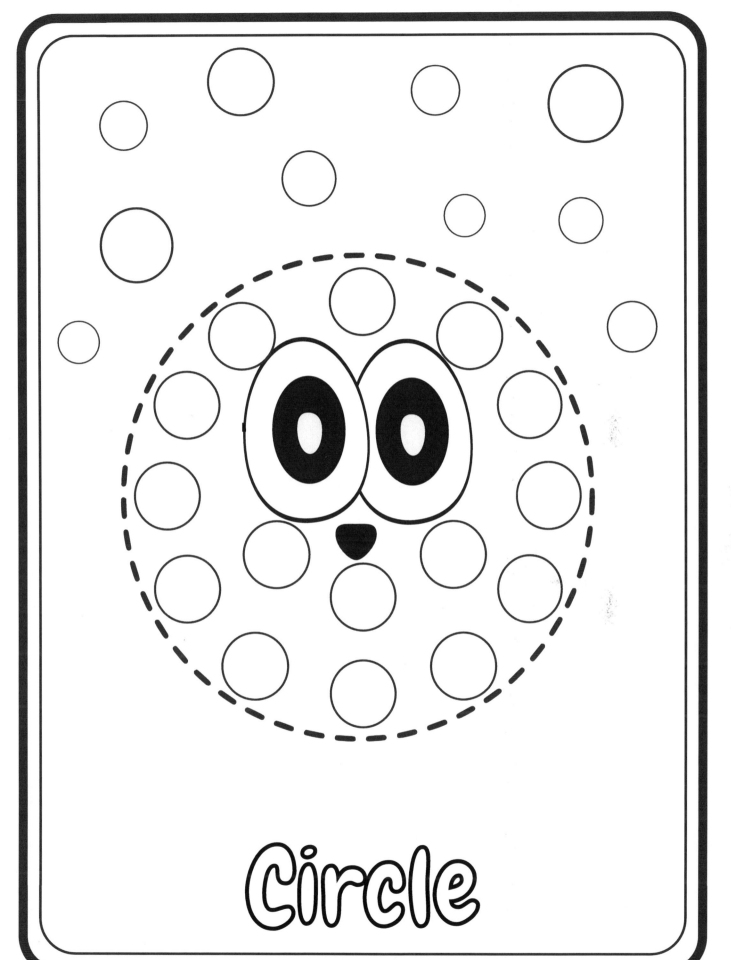

Circle

Triangle

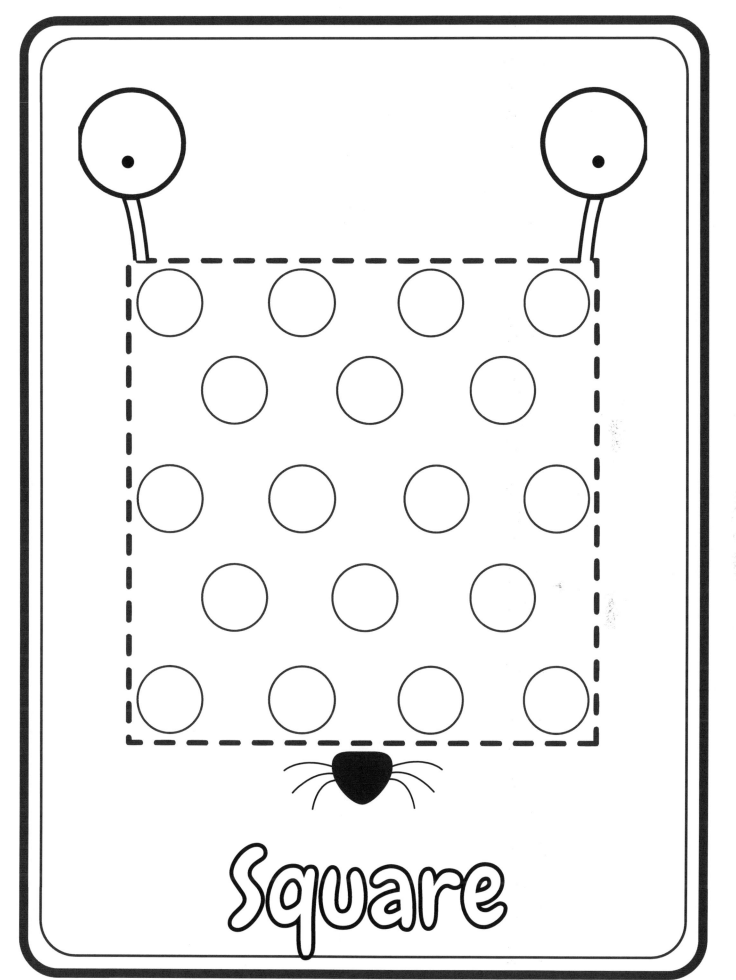

Square

Rectangle

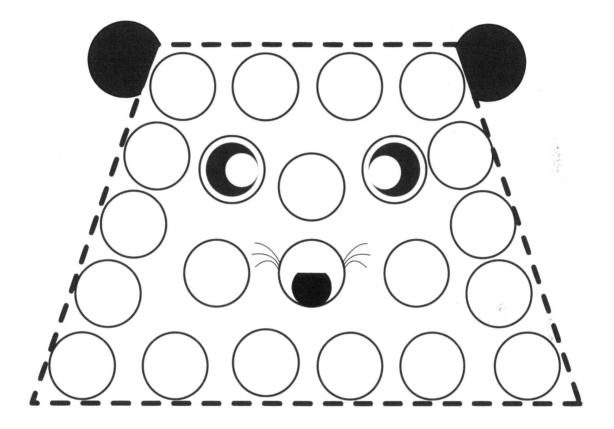

Trapezoid

Star

Oval

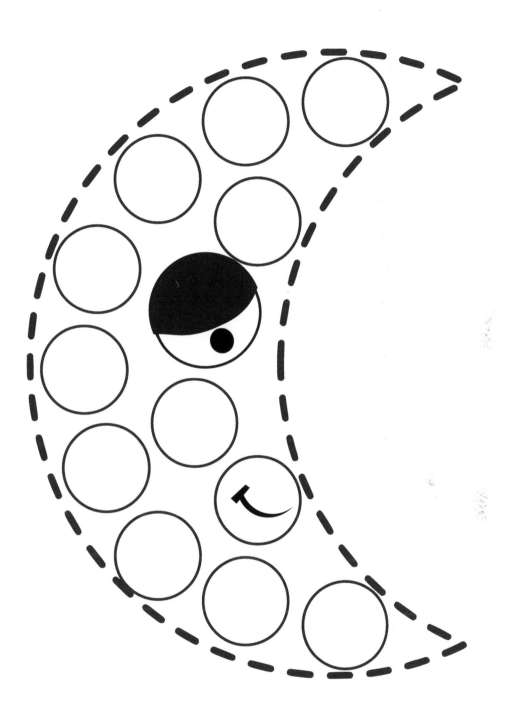

Crescent

Heart

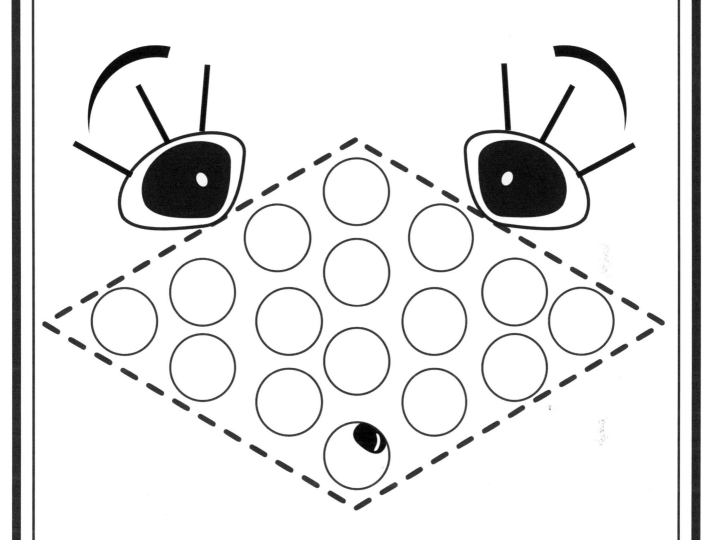

Diamond

I would be grateful if you could leave feedback about this book on Amazon :)

Printed in Japan
落丁、乱丁本のお問い合わせは
Amazon.co.jp カスタマーサービスへ